An integrated framework for mobile Ad Hoc Nework Security

Daniel Wa-Mbali

CIP a Camerei Naționale a Cărții

Wa-Mbali, Daniel.

An integrated framework for mobile Ad Hoc Nework Security / Daniel Wa-Mbali. – Chişinău : Generis Publishing, Rez.: lb. engl. – Bibliogr.: p. 41-42.

ISBN 978-9975-153-09-6.

004.7

W 37

Cover image: www.pixabay.com

Generis Publishing

Online orders: www.generis-publishing.com
Orders by email: info@generis-publishing.com

DEDICATION

To you my Parent for your love unexplainable sacrifice that I cannot measure to me your son.

ACKNOWLEDGEMENT

First of all we would like to thank the all mighty God for His countless blessings to complete our study. After that it is a great honour and privilege to thank our honorable project supervisor Dr. Elisha Ochla for his kind support and helpful supervision my CO-supervisor Dr. Stephen Akandwanaho throughout our study work that made us able to accomplished our goal. We express our heartfelt gratitude to him.

In addition we would like to thank our parents who always encourage us and push us to work Hard. It is our pleasure to say thanks to Pastor Kiluba WA kiluba, Pastor Alain, and all men of God support us in prayer.

We say thanks to my lovely wife Maisha Mangamba–mwangalalo and our children Grace lwamba-bihanga, Miriam Pombo Wa-mbali, Narcisse Mwangalalo Wa-mbali, Divine Mukebwa Wa-mbali, Emmanuel Afeka Mwangalalo for they sacrifice so this work can be done.

I would like to express my sincere gratitude to Leon Govender; Gideon for they assistance during this moment without forget all of ours friends and the seniors who guided us and helped us throughout this time.

ACRONYMS

IT: Information Technology
QoS: Quality of Service
PC: Personal Computer
SA: South Africa
LAN: Local Area Network
WPA: Wifi Protected access
WEP: wired equivalent privacy
UNISA: university of South Africa
IS: Information Systems
NCW: Network Centric Warefare
PAN: Personal area network
LAN: local area network
NS2: network simulator
AODV: Ad hoc on-demand distance vector routing
PDAs: personal digital assistants
MANET: Mobile ad hoc network
AP: the access point
BSS: basic service set
ODL: open distance learning
DoS: Denial-of-Service

ABSTRACT

In recent years, major changes have occurred in the world economy, in particular with regards to internet access. The development of internet access in the world about sharing information and wireless fast becoming accepted to maintain high-availability of internet so that internet connection for keeping connection up and available at all the time. For avoiding" putting all the eggs in one basket". The world has an integrated and unified place where almost a wide array of problems can be resolved by sharing information .The sharing of information as an IT service product and to generate a specific model for the IT unit, the process of the packaging of IT service that can help the users at the time they access the internet can improving users experience. For instance, students always complain that their connectivity was cancel due to infrastructure; it will be commendable to upgrade the quality of satisfaction of the user's Network usage

Keywords: Keywords- Mobile ad hoc network (MANET), Black hole, Packet dropping, Malicious node, Routing

TABLE OF CONTENTS

CHAPTER ONE

1.1 Introduction and background of the study

In recent years, wireless communication is one of the fastest-growing technologies. The demand for connecting devices without the use of cables is increasing everywhere. Wireless LANs can be found on college campuses, in office buildings, and in many public areas. In that case we can distinguish two types of basic service set .A basic service set as the building block of a wireless LAN, the mobile wireless station is known as the access point (AP). The BSS without an AP is a stand-alone network and cannot collaborate with other BSSs and them it called an ad hoc architecture that cannot need to have an access point and .A BSS with an AP is sometimes referred to as an infrastructure network.

A basic service set without an AP it's called an ad hoc network. Explosive growth of mobile computing devices, which mainly include laptops, personal digital assistants (PDAs) and handheld digital devices, has impelled a revolutionary change in the computing world: computing will not merely rely on the Capability provided by the personal computers, and the concept of ubiquitous computing emerges and becomes one of the researched hotspots in the computer science society .In this context, the availability of computer networks are vital since the incidents, however small, are immediately perceived by end users. The term "availability" is defined as the probability set up anywhere and anytime, without using any pre-existing network infrastructure that a service is in operation during a given time or what is the percentage of time during which a service is available, and not only be connected or available and be secure, according to ideas we have to secure our network even small it is we must follow some critical components that define security firstly confidentiality, access, integrity, and nonrepudiation. "A network is not only logically vulnerable but is also physically at risk physical security address the day-to-day security of a network no matter small or big it is .A set of networks security policies and procedures need to be defined that addresses organizational vulnerabilities. Security access is to be determined by such factors as who you are, what you do, what resources you require, and why" .Manufacturers have therefore worked to implement mechanisms to improve the convergence time of the network devices. In the ubiquitous computing environment, individual users utilize, at the same time, several electronic platforms through which they can access all the required information whenever and wherever maybe. The nature of the ubiquitous computing has made it necessary to adopt wireless network as the interconnection method: it is not possible for the ubiquitous devices to get wired network link whenever and wherever they need to connect with other ubiquitous devices. The Mobile Ad Hoc Network is one of the wireless networks that have attracted most concentrations from many researchers.

A Mobile Ad hoc Network (MANET) is a system of wireless mobile nodes that dynamically Self- organize in arbitrary and temporary network topologies. People and vehicles can thus be internetworked in areas without a pre-existing communication infrastructure or when the use of such infrastructure requires wireless extension. In the mobile ad hoc network, nodes can directly communicate with all the other nodes within their radio ranges; whereas nodes that are not in the direct communication range use intermediate node(s) to communicate with each other. In these two situations, all the nodes that have participated in the communication. Automatically form a wireless network. Therefore this kind of wireless network can be viewed as mobile ad hoc network. The mobile ad hoc network has the following typical features

1.2   Background of the study/ sector to be studied

2.1   UNISA – A brief background

Found in1873 as the university of the cape of Good hope, the University of south Africa (or UNISA as it is commonly known) spent most of is earl history as an examining agency for Oxford and Cambridge universities and as an incubator from which most other universities in south Africa are descended, In 1946, it was given a new role as a distance education university and today I offers certificate, diploma and degree courses up to doctoral level (ODL). University of south Africa (UNISA ,pronounced you-nee-sah) is the largest university on the Africa continent and attracts a third of all higher education student headcount of over 300,000 students in 130 countries worldwide, making it one of the world's mega universities.

Open distance learning entails a student-centered approach that gives students flexibility and provides them with extensive student support. Unisa is qualified like an comprehensive university, because for the vocational and academic programmes, many of which have received international accredition, as well as an extensive geographical footprint, giving their students recognition and employability in many countries the world over and its will be shown that is rated as one of the top universities in south Africa according market research. And the University has seven regional centers in South Africa, and its according provinces partition are these:

- Limpopo (Gani, Makhdo, Polokwane)
- Eastern Cape(East London, Mthatha, Por Elizabeth)
- Gauteng(Ekurhuleni, Florida, Johannesburg, Preoria, Vaal Triangle)
- Kwazulu-Natal(Durban, New Castle, Pietermaritzburg, Richards Bay, Wild Coast)

- Midlands(Bloemfontein,Kimberle,Mafikeng,Potchefstroom,Rustenburg)
- Mpumalanga(Middelburg, Nelspruit)
- Western Cape(Cape town, George)

And main campus in Muckleneuck, Pretoria we found also some office in different provinces, without forget kwa-zulu Natal office at Durban Main campus that will be our case of study (http://en.wikipedia.org/wiki/University_of_South _Africa (access 2014/07/29)).

1.3   Problem statement

Indeed the widespread use of the internet access everybody need to be allow to the internet connection under different topology we have a challenges in using mobile ad hoc network security threats according this technology the mobility affect signal transmission that overturn the communication, even causes route changes by affecting the channels access while limited wireless bandwidth in reducing network performance by black hole attacks. This project involves a literature survey and critical analysis on the current existing research work with regard to security issues in Mobile Ad Hoc Networks, as well as the possible solutions to the identified security issues.

Mobility and portability of wireless communication devices in mobile ad hoc networks introduce data security threats. This is due to the utilization of multiple hops as a result of limited transmission ranges, between source and destination nodes.(we found the students using lab computer that is not enough because the number of student is big, and student usually study in having group of study. After observation and receiving the complained for the student; there have an slow connection we need to design one system that can maintain the client in using internet access without infrastructure) The performance of MANET under Black Hole attacks can be improved by accurately detecting and eliminating Black Hole nodes. That is, there are indications to suggest that inaccurate Black Hole attack detection and elimination in mobile ad hoc networks have led to a low network performance

From the above encountered problems the following question have been asked research questions

1.4   Scope of the project

Research area for new information technologies and communication, mainly computers and internet will be the focus. As the subject suggests, the work is limited to Mobile Ad Hoc Network Security. The academy is located in the premises of the main campus; kwazulu-natal province in the city of Durban. Our research period will extend from the beginning to the end of the academic year March 2014-January2015.

1.5 Research aim

The aim of the research is to develop a secure routing algorithm in mobile wireless ad hoc networks:

To examine various methodological and substantive considerations in detecting and eliminating Black Hole attacks in ad hoc networks.

To conduct extensive literature review on the security issues in wireless mobile ad hoc networks as a result of routing algorithms used.

To investigate (by means of literature review in routing approaches/theories) what interventions are currently being undertaken to address mobile ad hoc network security threats.

To investigate (by means of theoretical analysis) how optimization can be used to select threshold values in attempts to secure mobile ad hoc networks through accurate identification of attackers.

To make recommendations on the type of routing approaches that can improve security in mobile ad hoc networks. To develop and simulate the proposed approach.

To make simulation comparisons of the proposed approach with the existing approaches (specifically in AODV routing), justifying the appropriateness.

1.6 Research questions

The following research questions can systematically lead to the research problem solutions:

- What effect does Black Hole attacks have on mobile ad hoc networks' routing security goals?

- What are the strengths and weaknesses of the current existing solutions to Black Hole attacks in mobile ad hoc networks?

- What impact does Black Hole attacks have on mobile ad hoc networks' routing performances?

- Can the utilisation of optimal threshold values improve accurate Black Hole node detection in mobile ad hoc networks?

•   How do you found that technologies in time of accessibility?

1.7 Hypothesis

A hypothesis is a proposed like transition to the series of answers to the issues raised in the problem. In another way it is defined as a proposal for the explanation of natural phenomena and should be verified by the facts. So, to solve the issues raised in the problem it is proposed: Mobile Ad Hoc Network security.

1.8 Independent variable

Construct a new network architecture and improve its performance by using a system of comparing different result, network architecture tuning, reducing bottlenecks performance and the strengths of the system.

1.9 Dependent variable

Establish whether a well-designed network architecture will maximize the infrastructures network between the users spends on the network – user satisfaction.

1.10 Organization of the study

Chapter 1 is the introduction of our work and explains application area, motivation, our aim, Background of the project, Problem statement, demarcation, Hypothesis, dependent and independent variables, Chapter 2 will explain the Literature Review, chapter3 explain the methodology used to achieve the work, chapter 4 Describe how data was collected for this study, how was it captured and recorded and the problems faced during distribution of questionnaires with provided solutions. Chapter 5 is about the practical work of our research and analyse the results for the whole project and the discussions, chapter 6 is the conclusion for our work.

CHAPTER 2

LITERATURE REVIEW

1. Introduction

1.1 Overview

This literature review provides a summary of research into the mobile Ad hoc Network Security. Establishment availability of communication. These technologies will be looked at to see how they can provide a guaranteed service for different types of traffic in a network.

1.2. Discussion concepts

A mobile ad hoc network (MANET) is a collection of autonomous nodes that communicate with each other by forming a multi-hop radio network and maintaining connections in a decentralized manner. Security remains a major challenge for these networks due to their features of open medium, dynamically changing topologies, reliance on cooperative algorithms, absence of centralized monitoring points, and lack of clear lines of defense. Most of the routing protocols for MANETs are thus vulnerable to various types of attacks. Ad hoc on-demand distance vector routing (AODV) is a very popular routing algorithm. However, it is vulnerable to the well-known black hole attack, where a malicious node falsely advertises good paths to a destination node during the route discovery process. This attack becomes more sever when a group of malicious nodes cooperate each other. In this paper, a defense mechanism is presented against a coordinated attack by multiple black hole nodes in a MANET. The simulation carried out on the proposed scheme has produced results that demonstrate the effectiveness of the mechanism in detection of the attack while maintaining a reasonable level of through put in the network. In this paper, routing security issues in MANETs are discussed in general, and in particular the cooperative black hole attack has been described in detail. A security protocol has been proposed that can be utilized to identify multiple black hole nodes in a MANET and thereby identify a secure routing path from a source node to a destination node avoiding the black hole nodes. As a future scope of work, the proposed security mechanism may be extended so that it can defend against other attacks like resource consumption attack and packet dropping attack. Adapting the protocol for efficiently defending against gray hole attack- an attack where some nodes switch their states from black hole to honest intermittently and vice versa, is also an interesting future work (Tata Consultancy Services Ltd.2011).

(A Mechanism for Detection of Cooperative Black Hole Attack in Mobile Ad Hoc Networks), Wireless Ad-hoc Network is a temporary and decentralized type of wireless network. Due to security vulnerabilities in the routing protocol currently, this type of network is unprotected to network layer attacks. Black-hole attack is such a type of attack and is a Denial-of-Service (DoS) attack. Due to its nature, the attack makes the source node send all the data packets to a Black-hole node that ends up dropping all the packets. The aim of this paper is to reflect light on the severe effects of a Black-hole attack in a Wireless Ad-hoc network and the drawbacks of the security mechanisms being used for the mitigation of this attack Wireless Ad-hoc networks have the ability to deploy a network where a traditional network infrastructure environment cannot possibly be deployed. With development in computing environments, the services based on ad hoc networks have been increased. Although many solutions for black-hole attack mitigation have been proposed but still these solutions are not perfect in terms of effectiveness and efficiency. In our study we analyzed the results of various simulations that ran black-hole attack in wireless ad-hoc network and the effect of this attack on packet delivery. Based on our research and analysis we draw the conclusion that the drop rate of packets is very high when there is a black-hole node present in the network and that the detection of black hole nodes in ad hoc networks is still considered to be a challenging task. An ad hoc wireless network is a collection of wireless mobile nodes that self-configure to construct a network without the need for any established infrastructure or backbone. Ad hoc networks use mobile nodes to enable communication outside wireless transmission range. Due to the absence of any fixed infrastructure, it becomes difficult to make use of the existing routing techniques for network services and this poses a number of challenges in ensuring the security of the communication. Many of the ad hoc routing protocols that address security issues rely on implicit trust relationships to route packets among participating nodes. The general security objectives like authentication, confidentiality, integrity, availability and nonrepudiation, the ad hoc routing protocols should also address location confidentiality, cooperation fairness and absence of traffic diversion. In this paper we attempt to analyze threats faced by the ad hoc network environment and provide a classification of the various security mechanisms. Mobile ad-hoc networks have properties that increase their vulnerability to attacks. Unreliable wireless links are vulnerable to jamming and by their inherent broadcast nature facilitate eavesdropping.

Constraints in bandwidth, computing power, and battery power in mobile devices can lead to application specific trade-offs between security and resource consumption of the device.

Mobility/Dynamics make it hard to detect behaviour anomalies such as advertising bogus routes, because routes in this environment change frequently. Self-organization is a key property of ad-hoc networks. Besides authentication, Confidentiality, integrity, availability, access control, and non repudiation being harder to enforce because of the properties of mobile ad-hoc networks, there are also additional requirements Such as location confidentiality, cooperation fairness and the absence of traffic diversion. The lack of infrastructure and of an organizational environment of mobile ad-hoc networks offers special opportunities to attackers. Without proper security, it is possible to gain various advantages by malicious behaviour: better service than cooperating nodes, monetary benefits by exploiting incentive measures or trading confidential information; saving power by selfish behaviour; preventing someone else from getting proper service, extracting data to get Confidential information and so on. Routes should be advertised and set up adhering to the routing protocol chosen and should truthfully reflect the knowledge of the topology of the network. By diverting the traffic towards or away from a node, incorrect forwarding, no forwarding at all, or other noncooperative behaviour, nodes can attack the network. We have discussed the various routing and forwarding attacks in this survey. We have also discussed prevention and detection mechanisms that were adopted to provide security in ad hoc networks. A prevention-only strategy will only work if the prevention mechanisms are perfect; otherwise, someone will find out how to get around them. Most of the attacks and Vulnerabilities have been the result of bypassing prevention mechanisms. In view of this reality, detection and response are essential. In this paper we discussed proposals representing all of these classes. Even though prevention works as the first line of defense, it is not sufficient in addressing all the security threats. Hence we suggest an integrated layered framework which adopts the prevention techniques for the first level and detection techniques can be used at the second level complementing the protection techniques (C. Sreedhar et al.2010).

Mobile Ad-hoc networks are a collection of mobile hosts that communicate with each other without any infrastructure. Due to security vulnerabilities of the routing protocols, wireless ad hoc networks may be unprotected against attacks by the malicious nodes. One of these attacks is the Black Hole Attack against network integrity absorbing all data packets in the network. Since the data packets do not reach the destination node on account of this attack, data loss will occur. In this paper are doing simulation study of network under black hole attack and do comparison with the network without attack working on AODV protocol using various performance metrics such as throughput, PDF and End to End delay in three different scenarios. In this paper we have analyzed the performance of ad hoc network under the black hole attack and compared that with the network without any attack working using AODV routing protocol in three scenarios (Monika Roopak, Dr. Bvr Reddy, August-2011.

MANET is a network of mobile nodes without any infrastructure. Due to its dynamic in nature MANET are at more risk to attacks. There are several attacks in MANET. Black Hole attack is one of the attacks that advertise it for having the shortest path to destination node and drops the entire packet that is coming from source node. In this paper, we have reviewed different IDS based solutions against Black hole attacks in Mobile Ad-Hoc networks and thoroughly compare these schemes to find out their various advantages and disadvantages. After it was been defined AODV protocol in MANET and the various authors have given several proposals for detection and prevention of black hole attacks in MANET but every proposal has its own disadvantages in their respected solutions and we made a comparison among the existed solutions. We observe that the mechanisms detects black hole node, but no one is reliable procedure since most of the solutions are having more time delay, much network overhead because of newly introduced packets and some mathematical calculations. For future work, to find an effective solution to the black hole attack on AODV protocol (Sarita Badiwal et al, May 2013),a mobile ad hoc network (MANET) is an autonomous network that consists of mobile nodes that communicate with each other over wireless links. In the absence of a fixed infrastructure, nodes have to cooperate in order to provide the necessary network functionality. One of the principal routing protocols used in Ad hoc networks is AODV (Ad hoc on demand Distance Vector) protocol. The security of the AODV protocol is compromised by a particular type of attack called 'Black Hole' attack. In this attack a malicious node advertises itself as having the shortest path to the node whose packets it wants to intercept. In this paper, their address the problem of coordinated attack by multiple black holes acting in group. And we propose a complete protocol to detect a chain of cooperating malicious nodes in an ad hoc network that disrupts transmission of data by feeding wrong routing information. And present a technique to identify multiple black holes cooperating with each other and a solution to discover a safe route avoiding cooperative black hole attack. In this paper we have studied the routing security issues of MANETs, described the cooperative black hole attack that can be mounted against a MANET and proposed a feasible solution for it in the AODV protocol. The proposed solution can be applied to

1.) Identify multiple black hole nodes cooperating with each other in a MANET; and

2) Discover secure paths from source to destination by avoiding multiple black hole nodes acting in cooperation. As future work, we intend to develop simulations to analyze the performance of the proposed solution. We also plan to study the impact of GRAY hole nodes (nodes which switch from good nodes to black hole nodes) and techniques for their identification (Mrs. M. Jhansi et all, August 2012).

There is no infrastructure in wireless ad hoc networks, and nodes independently manage the networks. Therefore, the connection between nodes is provided by the nodes themselves, and these nodes act as a router. In this case, they use routing protocol such as AODV. In order to provide the connections, nodes exchange data and control packages by trusting to each other. Since these networks have unique and special characteristics, they face with too much attack. One of these attacks is black hole attack in which destructive node attracts the network traffic, and destroys the packages. In this paper, black hole attack in AODV routing protocol has been investigated, and some solutions have been suggested. Simulation results indicate that, in proposed method, the rate of package delivery has been considerably increased in comparison with AODV. In this paper, a method has been proposed. In this method, according to behaviour of black hole, the method of selecting AODV responses changes in a way that the source node ignores the response received from black hole node, and sends data packages from another route. This can be done by allocating fidelity level to network node, changing the way of selecting response, updating and distributing fidelity table by the source node. They simulated five scenarios by NS2 simulator. At first, five scenarios were simulated without a black hole node, and then they were simulated with a blackhole node. The results indicate that our proposed method has increased delivery rate of package from 22, 32 percent to 42, and 34 percent in scenarios involving black hole. In this method, end-to-end delay and routing overhead is more than AODV due to waiting of the source node to collect response packages, more processing in comparison with AODV as well as general distribution of fidelity table (Iman Zangeneh et all, 2013)

Mobile Ad-hoc Network (MANET) is an autonomous system, where nodes/stations are connected with each other through wireless links. MANETs are highly vulnerable to attacks due to the open medium, dynamically changing topology, lack of centralized monitoring and management point. The possible and the commonest attack in ad hoc networks is the black hole attack. In the black hole attack, a malicious node advertises itself as having the shortest path to the destination node. In the existing method a detection method based on checking the sequence number in the Route Reply message by making use of a new message originated by the destination node was developed but the drawback here is that a malicious node can play a role of sequence number collector in order to get the sequence number of as many other nodes as possible. In this Research Paper, a system is being proposed via which the sequence number collector problem is overcome by classifying the nodes into three categories based on the behaviour. The malicious node is isolated from the active data forwarding and routing. The association between the nodes is used for the route selection. The scheme which is proposed in this research paper not only increases the routing security but also make the nodes cooperate among each other in the ad hoc network. In this paper we have discussed the characteristics of mobile ad hoc network and about the Black hole attacks. The proposed scheme of Association based AODV protocol increases the routing security and also encourages the nodes to cooperate in the ad hoc structure. It identifies the malicious nodes and isolates them from the active data forwarding and routing. Since the black hole node is the one which do not forward any message to the destination and consumes the entire message our proposed scheme identifies more than one black hole attacker node and the data is not allowed to pass through the black hole node path thus delay and overhead in route selection is reduced. (Anand Nayyar, June 2012). A mobile ad-hoc network (MANET) is an autonomous wireless network which consists of mobile nodes that communicate with each other over multi-hop wireless links. Due to the absence of any fixed infrastructure, MANETs are unprotected to various types of security attacks. Black hole is one of these attacks. Black hole is a type of routing attack where malicious nodes advertise itself as having the shortest path to all nodes in the environment by sending fake route reply. By doing this, the malicious node can deprive the traffic from the source node. There are lots of detection and defense mechanisms to eliminate the intruder that carry out the black hole attack. Here, a mechanism is proposed for the nodes which are deployed in MANETs in order to detect and prevent black hole attacks in this paper, we have surveyed and compared the existing solutions to black hole attacks on AODV protocol. The various authors have given several proposals for detection and prevention of black hole attacks in MANET but every proposal has its own disadvantages in their respected solutions and we made a comparison among the existed solutions. We observe that the mechanisms detects black hole node, but no one is reliable procedure since most of the solutions are having more time delay, much network overhead because of newly introduced packets and some mathematical calculations. For future work, to find an effective solution to the black hole attack on AODV protocol. (Khushbu Patel, February-2014 Mobile Ad hoc Networks (MANET) is a self-configuring, infrastructure less network consists of independent mobile nodes that can communicate via wireless medium.

Each mobile node can move freely in any direction, and changes their links to other devices frequently. Security is an essential part of ad hoc networks. Due to its dynamic topology, resource constraints, no centralized infrastructure and limited security, it is vulnerable to various attacks and black hole attack is one of them. In this attack, the malicious node advertises itself as having the shortest path to the destination and falsely replies to the route requests, and drops all receiving packets. In this paper, a mechanism to detect the multiple black hole nodes has been proposed by modifying AODV protocol. This paper is an enhancement to the AODV protocol by proving more security after detecting the single or multiple black hole nodes in MANET. By using fake RREQ packet and modified RREP packet, the multiple black hole nodes are detected at the initial stage before the actual route discovery process of AODV. It leads to less routing overhead and high packet delivery ratio. The parameters like PDR, end to end delay is used for checking if packets are dropped again or not, so that again detection can be done. So, whenever there is change in PDR and end to end delay as compare to average PDR and average end to end delay, there is need to detect the malicious node. In future, we will implement this mechanism in network simulator (NS2). And also, do experiments in enhancing the AODV protocol to detect the cooperative black hole and gray hole attacks, (International Journal for Technological Research in Engineering February-2014).

.In this paper, we discuss security issues and their current solutions in the mobile ad hoc network. Owe to the vulnerable nature of the mobile ad hoc network, there are numerous security threats that disturb the development of it. We first analyze the main vulnerabilities in the mobile ad hoc networks, which have made it much easier to suffer from attacks than the traditional wired network. Then we discuss the security criteria of the mobile ad hoc network and present the main attack types that exist in it. Finally we survey the current security solutions for the mobile ad hoc network. In this survey paper, we try to inspect the security issues in the mobile ad hoc networks, which may be a main disturbance to the operation of it?

Due to the mobility and open media nature, the mobile ad hoc networks are much more prone to all kind of security risks, such as Information disclosure, intrusion, or even denial of service. As a result, the security needs in the mobile ad hoc networks are much higher than those in the traditional wired networks. First we briefly introduce the basic characteristics of the mobile ad hoc network. Because of the emergence of the concept pervasive computing, there is an increasing need for the network users to get connection with the world anytime at anywhere, which inspires the emergence of the mobile ad hoc network. However, with the convenience that the mobile ad hoc networks have brought to us, there are also increasing security threats for the mobile ad hoc network, which need to gain enough attention. We then discuss some typical and dangerous vulnerabilities in the mobile ad hoc networks, most of which are caused by the characteristics of the mobile ad hoc networks such as mobility, constantly changing topology, open media and limited battery power. The existence of these vulnerabilities has made it necessary to find some effective security solutions and protect the mobile ad hoc network from all kinds of security risks. Finally we introduce the current security solutions for the mobile ad hoc networks. We start with the discussion on the security criteria in mobile ad hoc network, which acts as guidance to the security-related research works in this area? Then we talk about the main attack types that threat en the current mobile ad hoc networks. In the end, we discuss several security techniques that can help protect the mobile ad hoc networks from external and internal security threats. During the survey, we also find some points that can be further explored in the future, such as some aspects of the intrusion detection techniques can get further improved. We will try to explore deeper in this research area.

(Wenjia Li and Anupam Joshi,(Security Issues in Mobile Ad Hoc Networks- A Survey).

Mobile ad hoc networks are typically designed and evaluated in generic simulation environments. However the real conditions in which these networks are deployed can be quite different in terms of RF attenuation, topology, and traffic load. Furthermore, specific situations often have a need for a network that is optimized along certain characteristics such as delay, energy or overhead. In response to the variety of conditions and requirements, ad hoc networking protocols are often designed with many modifiable parameters. However, there is currently no methodical way for choosing values for the parameters other than intuition and broad experience. In this paper we investigate the use of genetic algorithms for automated selection of parameters in an ad hoc networking system. We provide experimental results demonstrating that the genetic algorithm can optimize for different classes of operating conditions. We also compare our genetic algorithm optimization against hand-tuning in a complex, realistic scenario and show how the genetic .Algorithm provides better performance. The first conclusion we can draw from our work is that the values chosen for the different parameters of the networking algorithm make a big difference in the performance of the network. Furthermore, there is not a single set of parameters that is the best, since the performance of a set of parameters depends greatly on the conditions under which the network is operating. This makes the problem of selecting a good set of parameters an important and difficult one. A second conclusion is that automated parameter optimization produces significantly better parameter values than hand tuning, at least based on our preliminary, experiments. Hence, the automated approach is one well worth pursuing to greater levels of sophistication's third conclusion is that for automated parameter optimization to work best, the training data should represent the full range of operating conditions under which the parameters need to function. This need for sufficient quantity of representative training data is one that is not unique to this problem but is rather common to all forms of statistical estimation. The work we have described is just preliminary and suggests some possible future work. One potential future task is comparing the genetic algorithm optimization performance with other stochastic optimization algorithms such as simulated annealing or tabu search. While we only had opportunity to investigate one algorithm so far, it would be valuable to do a comparative Study of optimization techniques. A second future task is implementation of the capability to have multiple machines running evaluations of different parameters simultaneously. An important feature of genetic algorithms is the ability to achieve approximately linear speedups via parallel evaluations, and we should exploit this to speed the optimization runs. David Montana and Jason Redi, (Optimizing Parameters of a Mobile Ad Hoc Network Protocol with a Genetic Algorithm), a Wireless ad-hoc network is a temporary network set up by wireless mobile computers (or nodes) moving arbitrary in the places that have no network infrastructure. Since the nodes communicate with each other, they cooperate by forwarding data packets to other nodes in the network. Thus the nodes find a path to the destination node using routing protocols. However, due to security vulnerabilities of the routing protocols, wireless ad-hoc networks are unprotected to attacks of the malicious nodes. One of these attacks is the Black Hole Attack against network integrity absorbing all data packets in the network. Since the data packets do not reach the destination node on account of this attack, data loss will occur. There is lots of detection and defense mechanisms to eliminate the intruder that carry out the black hole attack. We simulated the black hole attack in various wireless ad-hoc network scenarios and have tried to find a response system in simulations. In this paper, we analyzed the effect of Black Hole in AODV network. For this we implemented an AODV protocol that behaves as Black Hole in NS2. Having simulated the black hole attack, we saw that the packet loss is increased in ad-hoc network. The Black Hole Attack affects the overall network connectivity and causes data loss in network Therefore to minimize the black hole effect, we implemented IDSAODV protocol .The IDSAODV protocol will improve the packet delivery ratio and minimize the data loss. The advantage of this approach is the implemented protocol does not make any modification in packet format hence can work together with AODV protocol. Another advantage is that the proposed IDSAODV does not require any additional overhead and require minimum modification in AODV protocol. (www.ijera.com Vol. 2, Issue4, July-August 2012) The principles of Network Centric Warfare (NCW) are at the heart of DoD transformation plans and are the driving concept of several high profile acquisition programs.

This paper addresses the question of what communications and networking technology breakthroughs are required to fully realize mobile ad hoc networking (MANET) and deliver on the promises of NCW at the tactical edge of our military forces in the 2025 timeframe. We begin with a review of the background and major principles of NCW to define the key characteristics a NCW enabled force must exhibit. Next, we examine the basic concepts of networks and networking in both the context of network theory and in the specific implementation of fixed wired and wireless computer networks. We then describe the characteristics and challenges of mobile ad-hoc networks in general, and the unique requirements for NCW MANETs specifically. The heart of the paper then examines trends in relevant technologies for MANETs in both the commercial and military spheres, highlighting where the trends converge or diverge. Finally, specific technology investment recommendations are offered to set the stage for the successful development of MANETs to implement the vision of NCW. The tenets of NCW are the fabric of the DOD's transformation efforts and the drivers for several of the Department's largest acquisition programs. By adapting a network-centric culture, Organizational structure, and doctrine, and by embracing information technology to interconnect all the components of the DOD enterprise, we can use the resultant shared situational awareness to achieve information superiority. This information superiority will enable agile employment of a lighter, leaner, more lethal combat enterprise that overwhelms any potential adversary before they respond. In order to achieve the totality of this vision, we must robustly connect not just the core C4ISR canters, but all of the sensors, soldiers, vehicles, and aircraft – the tactical war fighting nodes – as well. Achieving this tactical edge connectivity will depend on the development of significantly improved MANET technologies. Beginning with an examination of the fundamentals of networking and network theory, the Basics of wired and wireless computer networks were examined as a lead-in to the specific Advantages and disadvantages of MANETs. After defining the characteristics of an objective .MANET in terms of connectivity, bandwidth, survivability, and security, an analysis of the Challenges and projected trends in MANET related a technology was undertaken. Viewed from the vantage point of the year 2025, our review of challenges and trends in research on radios and networking identified several key enabling technologies that will be Critical to achieving the characteristics of our objective MANET. Specifically on the radio side, the foundational technology of software defined radios (SDR) was judged as being strongly supported by both the commercial and defense markets.

Achieving the necessary SDR capabilities envisioned for our 2025 timeframe is considered to be a low risk and does not require any additional funding beyond the levels already planned to support near term JTRS (Brent A. Et all, April 2007) ; a Wireless ad-hoc network is a temporary network set up by wireless mobile computers (or nodes) moving arbitrary in the places that have no network infrastructure. Since the nodes communicate with each other, they cooperate by forwarding data packets to other nodes in the network. Thus the nodes find a path to the destination node using routing protocols. However, due to security vulnerabilities of the routing protocols, wireless ad-hoc networks are unprotected to attacks of the malicious nodes. One of these attacks is the Black Hole Attack against network integrity absorbing all data packets in the network. Since the data packets do not reach the destination node on account of this attack, data loss will occur. There are lots of detection and defense mechanisms to eliminate the intruder that carry out the black hole attack. We simulated the black hole attack in various wireless ad-hoc network scenarios and have tried to find a response system in simulations. In this paper, we analyzed the effect of Black Hole in AODV network. For this we implemented an AODV protocol that behaves as Black Hole in NS2. Having simulated the black hole attack, we saw that the packet loss is increased in ad-hoc network. The Black Hole Attack affects the overall network connectivity and causes data loss in network.

Therefore to minimize the black hole effect, we implemented IDSAODV protocol

.The IDSAODV protocol will improve the packet delivery ratio and minimize the data loss. The advantage of this approach is the implemented protocol does not make any modification in packet format hence can work together with AODV protocol. Another advantage is that the proposed IDSAODV does not require any additional overhead and require minimum modification in AODV protocol. (Ranjeet Suryawanshi et all, July-August 2012).

1.3 Chapter summary

The above review of literature has traced, Mobile Ad Hoc Network Security from its meaning, the processes involved, benefits, reasons for failure to its advantages due to the current technological used at university of South Africa. The pivotal argument has been that the users or students are at the center of the success on any efforts by organizations to gain competitive advantage by using Mobile Ad Hoc Network Security.

CHAPTER 3

RESEARCH METHODOLOGY

3.   Introduction

As a top to this chapter, the researcher will introduce the broad categories of research and then give a focused attention on quantitative research. For the purposes of this study I wish to focus mainly on the quantitative research approach. The choice of a research approach is motivated by variables such as the nature of the study, the objectives that the study seeks to achieve, resource availability and time constraints.

3.1   Research strategy

A strategy is overall approach to answering research question. It has six strategies: survey, design and creation, experiment, case study, action research and ethnography. In that list will an experiment strategy will be used to test cause and effect relationships, seeking to prove or disprove a causal link between a factor and an observed outcome. An experiment is then designed to prove or disapprove the hypothesis, all factors that might affect the result are excluded from the study, other than the one factor that is thought to cause a particular outcome, like choose an experiment strategy because we have to think about the hypothesis to be tested, the variables to be controlled and measured, and internal and external validity. Because research start by developing a theory that can be tested empirically via an experiment. This statement is of the form' factor a cause B'and is known as a hypothesis.

There are also different kinds of experiments: true experiments, quasi-experiments and uncontrolled trials. Now for our work will used quasi-experiment.

3.2   Research methods

According definition we are the various procedures, schemes and algorithms used in research. All the methods used by a researcher during a research study are termed as research methods. They are essentially planned, scientific and value-neutral. They include theoretical procedures, experimental studies, numerical schemes, statistical approaches, etc. Research methods help us collect samples, data and find a solution to a problem. Particularly, scientific research methods call for explanations based on collected facts, measurements and observations and not on reasoning alone. They accept only those explanations which can be verified by experiments. (S. Rajasekar 2013)

3.2.1 Quantitative approach

Quantitative research approach produce outcome that can be used to appear or note numerical changes in measurable types of a population of focus; generalize to other, similar situations; provide explanations of predictions; and explain causal relationships. The fundamental philosophy underlying quantitative research is known as positivism, which is based on the scientific method of research. Measurement is necessary if the scientific method is to be used. The scientific method involves an empirical or theoretical basis for the investigation of populations and samples.

Hypotheses must be formulated, and observable and measurable data must be gathered. Appropriate mathematical procedures must be used for the statistical analyses required for hypothesis testing. Quantitative methods depend on the design of the study (experimental, quasi-experimental, and on-experimental). Study design takes into account all those elements that surround the plan for the investigation, such as research question or problem statement, research objectives, operational definitions, scope of inferences to be made, assumptions and limitations of the study, independent and dependent variables, treatment and controls, instrumentation, systematic data collection actions, statistical analysis, time lines, and reporting procedures. The elements of a research study and experimental, quasi-experimental, and no experimental designs are discussed here. Only Quasi-experimental designs are appropriate when random assignment of subjects to a group is not possible. Much of the research in education and psychology is conducted in the field or in classroom settings using intact groups. In such cases, researchers assign treatments randomly to nonrandomly selected subjects. The lack of full control and nonrandom assignment of subjects to groups pose threats to the internal and external validity of quasi-experimental designs. Matching may be used to control for the lack of randomization. In matching, researchers try to select groups that are as similar as possible on all important variables that may affect the outcomes of a study. Pretests are also recommended to control for lack of randomization. Similar scores on a pre-test administered to all groups indicate that the groups were matched adequately. There is no doubt that quasi-experiments are weaker than true experiments for making causal inferences; however, information resulting from quasi-experiments is usually better than no information at all. (Neil J. Salkind 2010)

In fact for this section the different advantages and disadvantages for using experiments strategy will be discussed. Especially for that case quasi-experiments will be used because there are often variable that the research cannot control and that might have caused the measured effect.

Advantages of experiments as a research strategy include:

1. They are a well-established strategy, seen by many as the most scientific and therefore most acceptable approach. Where people have not received any formal research methods training, this is often the only research strategy they know.

2. They are the only research strategy that can prove causal relationships.

3. Laboratory experiments permit high level of precision in measuring outcomes and analyzing the data. Laboratory experiments allow researchers to remain at their normal place of work, without the time and cost incurred in visiting field sites

Disadvantages of experiments include:

1. Laboratory experiments often create artificial situation, which are not comparable with real-world situation.

2. It's often difficult or impossible to control all those relevant variables. It is often difficult to recruit a representative sample of participants.

3. It is may be necessary to conceal from participants the purpose of the research so that they do not skew the result by for example, performing in the way they think you want they do. However, deception of participants is normally viewed as unethical.

3.3. Data collection and analysis

There are four main types of quantitative research designs. You will need to decide which one is most appropriate for our research questions. While there are many different investigations that can be done, a study with a quantitative approach generally can be described with the characteristics of one of the following four types: Descriptive, Correlation, Causal-Comparative/Quasi-Experimental, and True Experimental. For our work will choose Causal-Comparative because is the one can establish cause and effect will see at the description: Causal-comparative/quasi-experimental research attempts to establish cause-effect relationships among the variables. These types of design are very similar to true experiments, but with some key differences. An independent variable is identified but not demonstrated by the experimenter, and effects of the independent variable on the dependent variable are measured. The researcher does not randomly assign groups and must use ones that are naturally formed or pre-existing groups. Identified control groups exposed to the treatment variable are studied and compared to groups who are not. For other author you can see there are different kinds of data used in quantitative data analysis because different analysis techniques are suited to different kinds of data. We are particularly concerned with four different types: nominal, ordinal, interval, and ratio data. In that list we choose only Ordinal data, with ordinal data, number are allocated to a quantitative scale, for example, students could be ranked in terms of terms of their examination results, 1, 2, 3, for example .This time unlike nominal data, there is an order to the designated code number so some arithmetical operations are possible. We can tell which student did better than another student. However, the arithmetical operations are limited. We don't know how much better the first placed student was than the second, or the tenth, and so on. A common use of ordinal data is in categorizing responses. For example, the responses' Disagree strongly','Disagree','Neitheir agree', Agree strongly' might be coded 1,2,3,4 and5,respectively.Again you can see there is an order to the designated code number for each response,5 means greater agreement than4,for instance. But we cannot know by how much' strongly agree' (5) is greater than' Agree' (4).For ordinal data, the categories are ranked, but we don't know the differences or intervals, between each rank. This type of data is sometimes called ranked data. To see whether there is in fact a statistically significant difference we can use the independent group t-test.to use it, the sample must be uses be independent, that is, each student was tested only once. The independent group t-test uses the mean and SD of the two sets of data to calculate a figure that tells us the likelihood that any differences between the two sets of data are down to chance. We can performance is significantly different, that is whether the probability of the observed difference being down to chance is less than 1 in 20 ($p<0.005$).This test can be used with small sample sizes (<50), and the sample do not have to be the same size, so it will not matter if there were more students enrolled in the previous year than the current year. Alternatively, you might want to measure student performance at the beginning of a course, and then give the same test to the students at the end. For each student you would have pairs of data, the before and after score. To see whether any apparent difference in score is significantly different, you could use the dependent or matched pair t-test (Encyclopedia of Research Design Quantitative Research.2010). This looks at the means from each group (before and after) and the differences between the score.

3.4 Data sources and gathering methods

As we have already noted, although the survey research strategy is often assumed to be based on questionnaires, it can also use other data generation methods such as interviews, documents and observations for that research we decide to use questionnaire.

A good researcher will consider a questionnaire's content validity, construct validity and reliability.

3.5 Data collection population

UNISA university students <u>Sampling frame</u>
Durban campus Main

3.6 Sampling method

("Non-probability sample. This used when the research believes it is not feasible or necessary to have a representative sample. Perhaps the time and cost of obtaining one are too great. Sometimes researchers do not know enough about the population". (Briony J Oates 2006).

A group of students from UNISA – Academy will participate in the research. Therefore convenience sampling which is one of the Non-probability sampling methods will be used since sample units (which are students) were selected because they can be accessed easily and conveniently.)

<u>Sample size</u>

40 Students from Academy

For the purpose of this research, a questionnaire composing of two parts has been constructed. Part 1 of the questionnaire measures the accessibility (connection) quality of the website.
Part 2 of the questionnaire measures user satisfaction and customer loyalty.

After going through a website students will be given questionnaire to evaluate the system's accessibility and their level of satisfaction.
Questionnaire sample is included in appendices.

3.7 Validity and reliability in quantitative research

"Reliability and validity are tools of an essentially positivist epistemology."

It seems when quantitative researchers speak of research validity and reliability, they are usually referring to a research that is credible while the credibility of a qualitative research depends on the ability and effort of the researcher. Although reliability and validity are treated separately in quantitative studies, these terms are not viewed separately in qualitative research. Instead, terminology that encompasses both, such as credibility, transferability, and trustworthiness is used; it seems when quantitative researchers speak of research validity and reliability, they are usually referring to a research that is credible while the credibility of a qualitative research depends on the ability and effort of the researcher. Although reliability and validity are treated separately in quantitative studies, these terms are not viewed separately in qualitative research. Instead, terminology that encompasses both, such as credibility, transferability, and trustworthiness is used.

Ethical considerations

As a researcher, you have responsibilities to your research participants and that also includes considering ethical concerns that may be involved in your research. The context in which you will be working should be considered carefully, the aim of your research and the sensitivity of your topic. The question that will be asked for the interviews or surveys should not be traumatizing or make the respondent/participants uncomfortable. To ask the participants about experiences or humiliating question can also create distress and increase the anxiety between the participant and interviewer.

The key ethical issues that should be considered in this research are content, confidentiality, and accuracy.

Consent

Everyone who will participate in the study of Mobile Ad Hoc Network Security should have freely consented to participation, without being unfairly pressurized. The student and all the participants will be well-informed about what participation entails.

Confidentiality

It is important to measure confidentiality to be straightforward by only authorized people or systems can access protected data we must ensuring confidentiality can be difficult e.g who determine which people or systems are authorized to access the current system? By "accessing" data in that we mean that an authorized party can access a single bit? The whole collection? Can someone who is authorized disclose those data to other parties .we understand well confidentiality is a security property because we can relate computing e.g. to those preserving confidentiality in the real world. To preserve confidentiality, precision is sacrificed. Enforcing confidentiality also lead to unknowing access. Suppose a personnel specialist works at one level of access permission.

Accuracy

This accuracy includes the authenticity and fidelity of the data collected for the topic. The researcher should be as accurate as possible.

Data Analysis

Quantitative data means, or evidence, based on number. It is the main type of data generated by experiments and survey, although it can be generated by other research strategies too. It is primarily used analyzed by positivist research in that case we will used experiments.

For every question in the questionnaire there is an associated value.

Framework of infrastructure for a network UNISA

UNISA have an connection network call SANREAL connection and his infrastructure network in his building all the campus are managing got that now we realized entail university in all south Africa have got one main server where is configure a active directory and in each city are using telecom to be connected on Proxy server at Pretoria ,Durban main campus have in his building their have 30 AP and 3 computer labs join each one of them to switch that have 4 villain are belong for each users that means AP, Students, Staff, security.

AP: connection the Wi-Fi

Students via myunisa: where students can download study materials, etc... Staff: belong to all connections that can access no restrictions to them Security: that is only for security staff.

The University has seven regional centers in South Africa, and its according provinces partition are these?

- Limpopo (Gani, Makhdo, Polokwane)
- Eastern Cape (East London, Mthatha, Por Elizabeth)
- Gauteng (Ekurhuleni, Florida, Johannesburg, Preoria, Vaal Triangle)
- Kwazulu-Natal(Durban, New Castle, Pietermaritzburg, Richards Bay, Wild Coast)
- Midlands(Bloemfontein,Kimberle,Mafikeng,Potchefstroom,Rustenburg)
- Mpumalanga(Middelburg, Nelspruit)
- Western Cape(Cape town, George)

And like said on the presentation for our domain study all of them have the some topology or infrastructures and all replications are made at Pretoria no additional child-domain in this network every movement are control by an forest or tree-domain ;every ADDS infrastructure start with an single forest containing a single domain, there are a great many organizations, even very large one we realized that after create Active directory they have one domain primary and all replication are made there or here we have to study for Mobile ad hoc network wireless security and in the future will studying about configuration of an network at UNISA Proxy server .we have to concentrated in Mobile Ad hoc network wireless for this work.

Structure existents of network Wi-Fi=Protected by Password

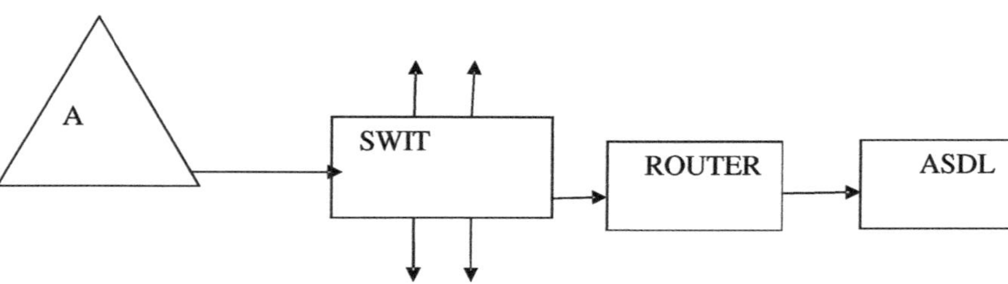

Fig 1: *Infrastructure existent for network Durban*

CHAPTER 4

RESEARCH FINDINGS AND DATA ANALYSIS

4.1 Introduction

In our chapter we have to present the data and results from analyzed and simulation. It also the result from the findings from this study in relation to existing research objectives supported by the questionnaire. First, the descriptive data will be presented and subsequently the data analysis relevant to each objective and survey questions will be presented and discussed. Finally Concerning security wireless networks there we have to see two main approaches to securing wireless networks such as Wi-Fi and wiMAX. Wired equivalent privacy (WEP) used to use encryption based on 64-bit key, which has been upgraded to a 128-bit key. WEP represents an early attempt at securing wireless communications and is not difficult for hackers to crack. Most wireless networks now use the WiFi protected Access (WPA) security protocol that offers significantly improved protection over WEP and that technique is only for wireless with access point now for these type of work regarding mobile ad hoc network security like says above its will be focus on basic set service without infrastructure (Ralph et al, Wireless Network annex) so a short summary of the results will be provided. The questionnaire, as refer indirectly to the previous chapter was divided into first sections and the first section will be in answering to the questions mention in chapter one and the second part it's will be make an simulation practical in putting a security routing in that wireless in mobile ad hoc.

- What effect does Black Hole attacks have on mobile ad hoc networks' routing security goals?

- What are the strengths and weaknesses of the current existing solutions to Black Hole attacks in mobile ad hoc networks?

- What impact does Black Hole attacks have on mobile ad hoc networks' routing performances?

- Can the utilization of optimal threshold values improve accurate Black Hole node detection in mobile ad hoc networks?

- How do you found that technologies in time of accessibility?

4.2 The different types of wireless topology

Wireless communication is one of the fast-growing technologies; the demand for connecting devices without the use of cables is increasing everywhere. Wireless LANs can be found on college campuses, in office buildings, and in many public areas. We put all together in two types of wireless technologies for LANs: IEEE802.11 wireless LANs. Although both protocols need several layers to operate.

4.3 IEEE 802.11 has defined the specifications for a wireless LAN, called IEEE 802.11, which covers the physical and data link layers.

Concerning architecture of the network wireless the standard defines two kinds of services: the basic service set (BSS) and the extended service set (ESS).

Basic Service Set

IEEE 802.11 defines the basic service set (BSS) as the building block of a wireless LAN.A basic service set is made of stationary or mobile wireless stations and an optional central base station, known as the access point(AP).we will see two types in that standard. A BSS with an AP is sometimes referred to as an infrastructure network. A BSS without an AP is a stand-alone network and cannot send data to other BSS.It is called an ad hoc architecture. In this architecture, stations can form a network without the need of an AP; they can locate one another and agree to be part of a BSS. A BSS sometimes referred to as an infrastructure network.

4.4 Briefly historique and application of Bluetooth

Bluetooth is a wireless LAN technology designed to connect devices of different functions such as telephones, notebooks, computer (desktop and laptop), cameras, printers, coffee makers, and so on. A Bluetooth LAN is an ad hoc network, which means that the network is formed spontaneously; the devices, sometimes called gadgets, find each other and make a network called a piconet. A Bluetooth LAN can even be connected to the internet if one of the gadgets that try to connect, there is chaos. Bluetooth technology has several applications, Peripheral devices such as a wireless mouse or keyboard can communicate with the computer through this technology. Monitoring devices can communicate with the sensor devices in a small health care center. Home security devices can use this technology to connect different sensor to the main security controller.

Conference attendees can synchronize their laptop computer at a conference. And today Bluetooth technology is the implementation of a protocol defined by the

IEEE802.15 standard. The standard defined a wireless personal area network (PAN) operable in an area the size of a room or hall. And according the architecture Bluetooth is defined in two types of network: piconet and scatternet. Here we just show some kind of topology that we have is not our topic let us go through in topic ()

4.5 Advantage and disadvantage of MANET Advantages/Disadvantages

Advantages

1. Independence from central network administration

2. Self-configuring, nodes are also routers

3. Self-healing through continuous reconfiguration

4. Scalable: accommodates the addition of more nodes

5. Flexible: similar to being able to go the Internet from many different locations

Disadvantages

Each node must have full performance.

1. Throughput is affected by system loading

2. Reliability requires a sufficient number of available nodes. That kind of networks can have problems

3. Large networks can have excessive latency (high delay), which affects some application.

4.6. Limitations of Manet technologies

According these technology it cannot allow a long distance of a connection to be connected to another devices or computer so the computer must be closer.

1. MOBILE Ad hoc Network Security

1.1.A Security Criteria

Before we study the solutions that can help secure the mobile ad hoc network, we think it Important to realize how we will conclude if a mobile ad hoc network is secure or not, or in Other words, what will be see in head of the security criteria for the mobile ad hoc network; Microsoft does not accepted advanced encryption and protocols security for wireless Ad hoc networks on <u>Windows</u>. Indeed, the security hole bring by Ad hoc networking is not only the Ad hoc network itself, but the bridge it determined into some networks.

When we want review officially the security state of the mobile ad hoc network. According that, we briefly introduce the widely-used criteria to examine if the mobile ad hoc network is secure.

1.2 Availability

That will our focus is one the key its show us like the system can solved the issue for ours student because the first system was not give accessibility to the network all the time when theirs need it, so we define availability like an essential tool which to perform particular tasks. But when the system is not available, busy serving other users or down to be repaired or upgraded the users are very aware of certain information's unavailability, finally, availability is important because of the shared access motivation underlying some information.

1.3 Integrity

The integrity is much harder to pin down, point out, integrity means different things in different contexts. When we survey the way some people use the term, we find several different meanings and can also mean two or more of these properties. Welke and Mayfield recognize tree particular aspect of integrity: authorized action, separation and protection of resources, and error detection and correction. Integrity can be enforced in much the same way as can confidentiality: by rigorous control of who or what can access which resources in what as some forms of integrity are well represented in the real world, and those precise representations can be implemented in a computerized environment.

1.4 Confidentiality

So we realized confidentiality is also important, because the protection has several aspects, in order to maintain the confidentiality of some confidential information, we need to keep them secret from all entities that do not have the privilege to access them.

1.5 Authenticity

Authenticity is essentially assurance that participants in communication are genuine and not Impersonators. It is necessary for the communication participants to prove their identities as what they have claimed using some techniques so as to ensure the authenticity. If there is not such an authentication mechanism, the adversary could impersonate a benign node and thus get access to confidential resources, or even propagate some fake messages to disturb the Normal network operation.

1.6 Nonrepudiation

Nonrepudiation ensures that the sender and the receiver of a message cannot disavow that they have ever sent or received such a message. This is useful especially when we need to discriminate if a node with some abnormal behavior is compromised or not: if a node recognizes that the message it has received is erroneous, it can then use the incorrect message as an evidence to notify other nodes that the node sending out the improper message should have been compromised.

1.7 Authorization

Authorization is a process in which an entity is issued a credential, which specifies the privileges and permissions it has and cannot be falsified, by the certificate authority.

Authorization is generally used to assign different access rights to different level of users. For instance, we need to ensure that network management function is only accessible by the network administrator. Therefore there should be an authorization process before the network administrator accesses the network management functions.

1.8 Anonymity

Anonymity means that all the information that can be used to identify the owner or the current user of the node should default be kept private and not be distributed by the node itself or the system software. This criterion is closely related to privacy preserving, in which we should try to protect the privacy of the nodes from arbitrary disclosure to any other entities. The internet and e- commerce add some challenging aspect to security-commerce require that portions of the computer system be available to consumers and other business, greater business benefits are generated when websites are integrated with corporate data such as inventory so customers can precised if an things is in stock. Yet, accepting public access to these systems creates greater security risk. Additionally, since the internet is a shared public network, data needs to be protected in transmission to ensure it is not intercepted or altered. Wireless networks are even more open to eavesdropping and interception. Because of the public nature the internet, even a well-protected system can be brought down with denial-of-service attacks. (George Werthman. Management information system 3third edition, page125).Since the network are facing with some attack we difference in two types: Internal and external attack in that is a challenge of keeping computer secure has never been greater, not only because number of attack, but also because of the difficulties faced I defending against these attack:

(i).   External attacks, in which the attacker goals to cause congestion, propagate fake routing Information or disturb nodes from providing services.

(ii).   Internal attacks, in which the enemies wants to gain the usually access to the network and participate the network movement, either by some malicious impersonation to get the access to the network as a new node, or by directly compromising a current node and using it as a basis to conduct its malicious behaviors.

In the two categories shown above, external attacks are similar to the normal attacks in the traditional wired networks in that the adversary is in the proximity but not a trusted node in the network, therefore, this type of attack can be prevented and detected by the security methods such as membership authentication or firewall, which are relatively conventional security solutions. However, due to the pervasive communication nature and open network media in the mobile ad hoc network, internal attacks are far more suspected than the internal attacks: because the destroys nodes are originally to the users of the ad hoc network security, they can easily go over the authentication and get protection from the security mechanisms. As a result, the adversaries can make use of them to gain normal access to the services that should only be available to the authorized users in the network, and they can use the legal identity provided by the compromised nodes to conceal their malicious behaviors. Therefore, we should pay more attention to the internal attacks initiated by the malicious insiders when we consider the security issues in the mobile ad hoc networks. In the following, we discuss the main attack types that emerge in the mobile ad hoc networks.

1.9 Denial of Service (DoS)

Denial of service attacks has gained a consideration in the last few years. The essence of an e- commerce site is the ability to reach customers 24 hours a day. If someone floods the site with meaningless traffic, then no one can use the service, and they may go out of business; In the traditional wired network, the DoS attacks are carried out by flooding some kind of network traffic to the target so as to exhaust the processing power of the target and make the services provided by the target become unavailable. Nevertheless, it becomes not practical to perform the traditional DoS attacks in the mobile ad hoc networks because of the distributed nature of the services. Moreover, the mobile ad hoc networks are more vulnerable than the wired networks because of the interference-prone radio channel and the limited battery power. In the practice, the attackers.

CHAPTER 5

IMPLEMENTATION AND DISCUSSION

5.1 Implementation

The information for our study has been collected in a form of questionnaires which were handed out to some participants, and it was captured using Microsoft Excel. The questions were close and open ended and each was assigned to a unique number.

E.g. Part 2, Q3 The system quickly responds to my input or clicks.

Table 4.1

Strongly Agree	Agree	Neutral	Disagree	Strongly Disagree
5	4	3	2	1

Each questionnaire will be assigned a unique identifier and it will be stored in Microsoft Excel

In table 4.2 above, five options will be assigned a unique value. All selected value(s) were captured for each participant and recorded using Microsoft Excel spreadsheet. E.g. If a participant select "Strongly Agree", Agree, Neutral, Disagree, Strongly disagree that follow the number mention in it row so to make the questionnaire the one is very approved by users.

Table 4.2

	A	B	C	D	E	F	G
1			Internet users satissfaction quantitative				
2			Part I		Part II		
3	ID#	Q5	Q4	Q1	Q2	Q3	
4	1	5	5	4	3	5	
5	2	2	3	4	2	2	
6	3	4	4	3	1	5	
7	4	1	2	2	2	4	
8	5	3	4	1	5	4	

5.2 Frequency, Value and Percentage table

Frequencies allow showing how many something will be occurred. Frequency table displays the frequencies and/or percentages of the response items for one question as the value giving to this connection. The number of times a certain response occurred for a specific question is counted using the MS Excel "count If" function. And the percentage (%) will be calculated using the formula below:

Percentage (%) = ((total number of responses) / (total number of individuals participated on each question))*100

Table 4.3

Q1 HOW Often do you access the internet?			
Response	Value	Frencency	Percentage
Once a month	1	2	3%
Once a week	2	9	15%
Several time a week	3	15	25%
Everyday	4	12	20%
Several time a day	5	22	37%
Total		60	100%

For each question, the number of times a value occurs is counted. Microsoft Excel "count If" function will be used to determine value frequencies.

Fig 2:

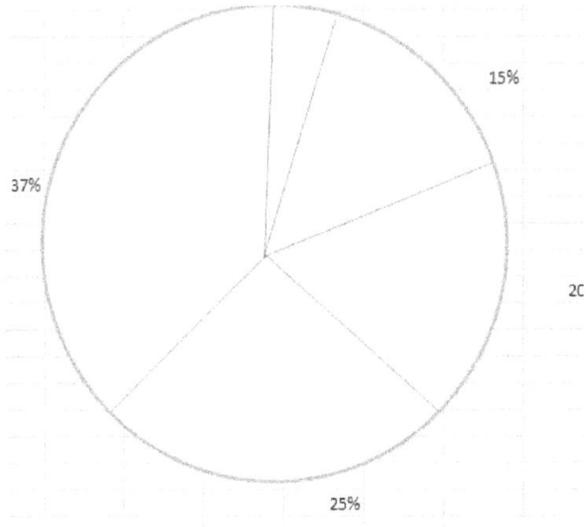

For clearer results the percentage column will be converted into a graph using Microsoft Excel.

5.3 Problems encountered and Solutions

• Most students they were refusing to answer the questioners saying that they don't have time because they were busy preparing their assignment and exams and it was hard for us to ask them some question. But we were trying our best to find them during time, while the discuss something else just for releasing.

• Some students their do not want to participate to research staff so they couldn't answered our questions and those incomplete questionnaires were discarded. We did buy packets of cheeps and biscuits for trying to make them to will to answer the questionnaires.

XIII. Diagrammatic representation Explanation for diagram

Firstly search a problem for the topic proposal, ask some questions to help collect data, and then I searched some important articles that emphasize about the same domain, a then I decided by choosing the research strategy and method which can help to solve problems encountered in my project by the end of the project and I will try to find the simulator that can solve that situation without any infrastructure

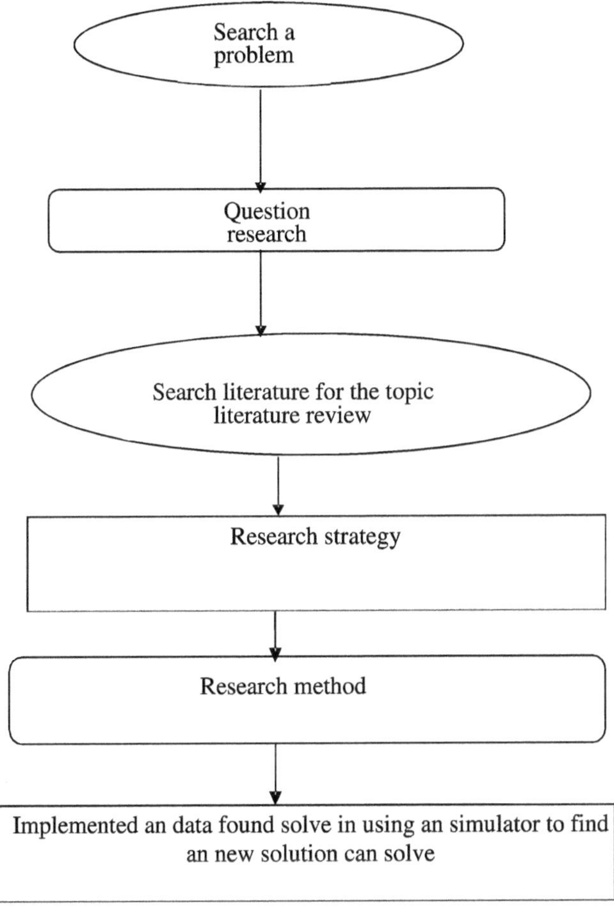

Fig 3: Diagrammatic representation how to project it was conducted

5.4 Conclusions

The research problem this study has sought to address is:

Mobile Ad Hoc Network Security a key to regaining its competitive advantage? Sharing information.

First, the findings of this study suggest that UNISA-Durban does not have a bandwich so large to support all the student they can be connected to internet connection, without interruption to the connection while there have an study group which is crucial regarding their study because the using ODL so them the connection is important (Chapter 4).

The second finding was that UNISA-Durban has fully embraced the use of internet connection to contact their lecture and follow student. The fact that that the organization tended to use internet connection as the main option of contact with their students means that it is losing out on the potential benefits of using internet as a way of contacting its student and follow student. Internet access have proved to be a cheap and effective way of communication and maintaining relationships with computer as found in the literature review. While the Internet may seem like an anonymous space, in reality it is far easier.

Indeed computing or information systems are growing fast because it is facing a big challenge in the world, the world need progress all the time and in all generations want to be closed that is why in the some way we need to solve that issue infrastructure network, to evaluate the easy connection without using the infrastructure, can be capable to solving problems.

In fact you can see with infrastructure network at many issues, is an advocacy organization to represent the "nuts and bolts" of the internet and plans roles in public policy development. This way will resolve the world the problems, here we make it ,in using some strategies and method to found an solution for the disconnection is happens while students study in group like scientific workers we can solve problem if use simulator and technical solutions to get the outcome response and need for students in academy.

CHAPTER 6

ANALYSIS OF RESULT AND DISCUSSION

6.1 Overview

This chapter describes the laboratory set-up of the Mobile Ad Hoc Network Security used for this study. The first section discusses the performance metrics to be evaluated. The next section covers the scope of the experimentation for this study. The chapter then presents the overall network architecture of the Mobile Ad Hoc Network Security laboratory setup and the basic configuration for the computer. This is followed by a detailed description of the various parameters of interest, the test cases and the required router configuration for the testing.

6.2 Scope of experiment

In order to identify the contributing factors to the time delay connectivity and packet loss of a network, and to determine the possible configuration options that could be used to reduce the time of connectivity, it is the interest of this study to examine some of the key components in mobile ad hoc networks. This means manipulating some of their parameters or attributes to see if they have direct impact on the impact of reduce the time. Some of the components to be investigated include the label distribution protocol and the mobile ad hoc networks. Due to time and resource constraints, it is not the aim of this study to examine each and every parameter/attribute of the various components of the detecting and eliminating Black Hole attacks in ad hoc networks.

However, through the initial literature research of this study work, the scope of the experimentation was limited to a few identified parameters for each component.

6.3 Tools

In our project we simulated our network using OMNET++4.5, this is a graphical network simulator that allows you to easily design network topologies and then run simulations on them. At the moment OMNET++4.5 supports Ad hoc routing; you can even extend your own network by connecting it to your ad hoc topology.

6.4 Laboratory SET-UP

Set-up in the laboratory. Mobile Ad Hoc Network Security is formed by 3 computers. Whose main functionality was to perform label self-configuration, were set up to form the core of the network without a backbone or any infrastructure. Three computers can communicate (PC1, PC2, and PC3) which were the main workhorse for this network without infrastructure; they formed the entry and exit points to the computer. Each computer (PC1, PC1, PC1) was connected to two Campus each one the computer for the follow students. Each Computer served as a link from the user's network to the service provider's network.

Fig 3

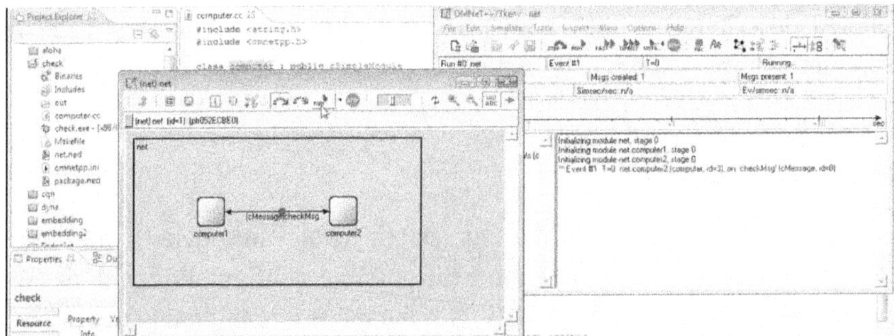

Fig 4

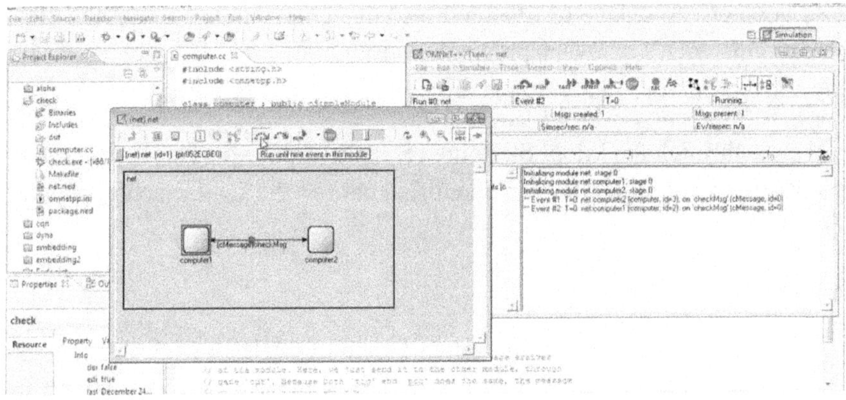

Fig 5

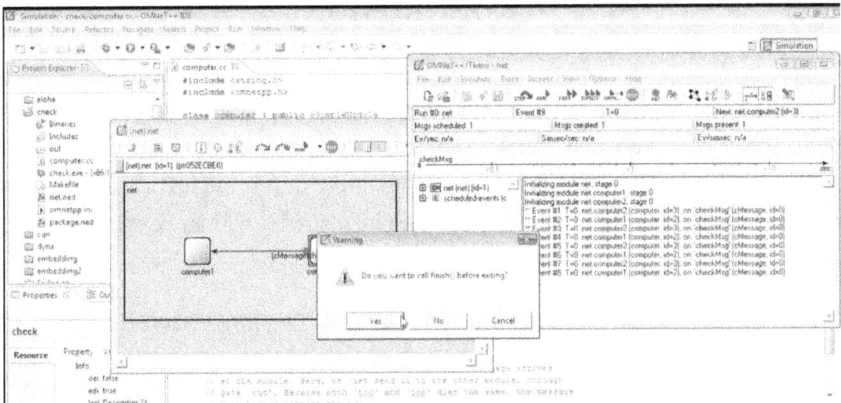

Fig 6

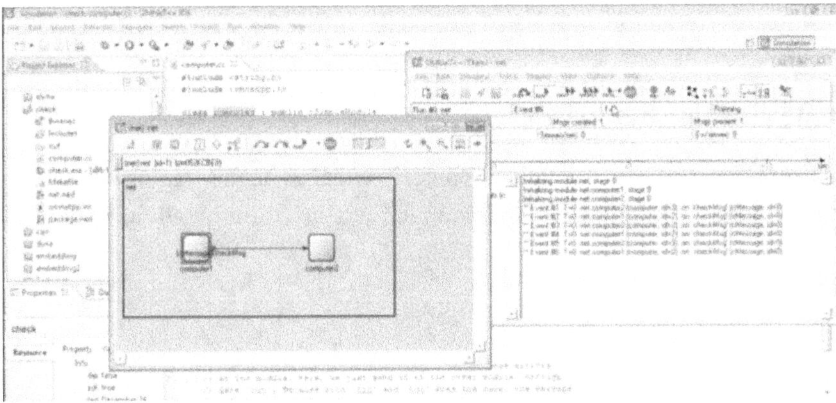

6.5 Results analysis

The test of laboratory it easy to configure because that I don't need any infrastructure to be set up, and the host can communicated without infrastructure so the need for the student will be answer.

CHAPTER 7

CONCLUSION

Indeed computing or information systems are growing fast because it is facing a big challenge in the world, the world need progress all the time and in all generations want to be closed that is why in the some way we need to solve that issue infrastructure network, to evaluate the easy connection without using the infrastructure, can be capable to solving problems.

In fact you can see with infrastructure network at many issues, is an advocacy organization to represent the "nuts and bolts" of the internet and plans roles in public policy development. This way will resolve the world the problems, here we make it ,in using some strategies and method to found an solution for the disconnection is happens while students study in group like scientific workers we can solve problem if use simulator and technical solutions to get the outcome response and need for students in academy.

7.1 Restrictions of this research

This research has no restrictions since it expands to all the universities of the country and computing sector is available in universities throughout the country.

7.2 Further use

This research is recommended in the planning of the university curriculum of any university that has computing qualification.

BIBLIOGRAPHY

Shireman, R. M. (2011, April 10). Redundancy in a community correction network. *Redundancy in a community correction network*, pp. 2-3.

All, M. B. (2008). *A guide for student in computer science and information system (Thesis Project)*. United Kingdom: digital Publishing solution second edition p135-142.

Cisco.com. (2013, April 15). IP sec VPN wan design overview. *IP sec VPN wan design overview*, pp. 1-3.

Close-up Media. (2012, September 29). AiNET introduces internet infrastructure i2 coalition. *AiNET introduces internet infrastructure i2 coalition*, p. 1.

Helen Menhenett. (2013, September 24). Head of Research, fairplace. *Head of Reseach, fairplace*, p. 1.

J.oates, B. (2006). *Researching Information System and computing (Reviewing the literature)*. London ECIYISP: in British library first Published, p71-72.

J. Shimonki, R. (2010, June 15). Important of Network redundancy. *Important of Network redundancy*, pp. 1-2.

Lithgow, M. (2007). *The roles of information and communication technologies.* Pietermaritzburg: Bibliotheoname seventh pp. 302-303.

M. Stair, R. (2006). *Principles of information systems management Approach (Principles of information systems)*. United States: Digital Publishing Solution seventh p302-303.

Miller's, D. (2010, August 10). Planning Networking forum. *Planning Networking forum*, p. 1.

Paessler. (2013). Up redundancy and auto-healing for your IT infrastructure. *Conference of the Dirty Paessler,* (pp. 1-2). Boston.

Pfleeger, C. P. (2011). *Security Networks (Security Computing)*. United State: Library of Congress Cataloging fourth.

Reynold, R. s. (2012). *Telecommunication and Networking the internet, web, internet, and extranets (information systems).* United States: Cencagage learning, tenth edition p216-300.

Tamarra Dean, T. (2013). *Network+, Guide to network.* United State: international Published sixth p195-365. TL, T. l. (2003). *Cisco.* United State of America: Neil Edde, fith Published, p257-449.

Wanredundancy.com. (2012, April 24). It and instrumention for industries. *It and instrumention for industries*, pp. 3-4.

Wayne.Goddard, W. a. (2005). *Research Methodology.* Berne: Berne Convention second Published p96-99.

www.amplicom.com. (2013, September 27). IT and instrumentation for industries. *IT and instrumentation for industries*, p. 3.

www.nova. (2013, September 27). Understanding reliability and validity in qualitative research. *Understanding reliability and validity in qualitative reseach*, pp. 2-4.

Appendix A

Code source Appendice simple computer
```
{
gates:
input in;
output out;
}


}


/

simple computer
{
gates:
input in;
output out;
}


//
// TODO documentation
//
network net
{
@display("bgb=351,276"); submodules:
computer1: computer {
@display("p=30,94");
}
computer2: computer {
@display("p=272,104");
}
connections:
computer2.out --> computer1.in; computer1.out --> computer2.in;
}


#include <string.h>
#include <omnetpp.h>
```

```cpp
class computer : public cSimpleModule
{
protected:
// The following redefined virtual function holds the algorithm.
virtual void initialize();

virtual void handleMessage(cMessage *msg);
};


Define_Module(computer);

void computer::initialize()
{


if (strcmp("computer", getName()) == 0)
{
cMessage *msg = new cMessage("checkMsg"); send(msg, "out");
}
}
void computer::handleMessage(cMessage *msg)
{

// The handleMessage() method is called whenever a message arrives
// at the module. Here, we just send it to the other module, through
// gate `out'. Because both `tic
' and `toc ' does the same, the message


// will bounce between the two. send(msg, "out");
}


/*

*computer.cc
*Created on: Dec 2, 2014
```

```cpp
* Author: Lusato

*/

#include <string.h> #include <omnetpp.h>

class computer : public cSimpleModule

{

protected:

// The following redefined virtual function holds the algorithm. virtual void initialize();

virtual void handle Message(cMessage *msgb);

};

Define_Module(computer);

void computer::initialize()

{

if (strcmp("computer", getName()) == 0)

{

cMessage *msg = new cMessage("checkMsg"); send(msg, "out");
}

}
```

```cpp
void computer::handleMessage(cMessage *msg)

{

// The handleMessage() method is called whenever a message arrives

// at the module. Here, we just send it to the other module, through

// gate `out'. Because both `tic' and `toc' does the same, the message

// will bounce between the two. send (msg, "out");
}
```

Appendix B

Fig 1

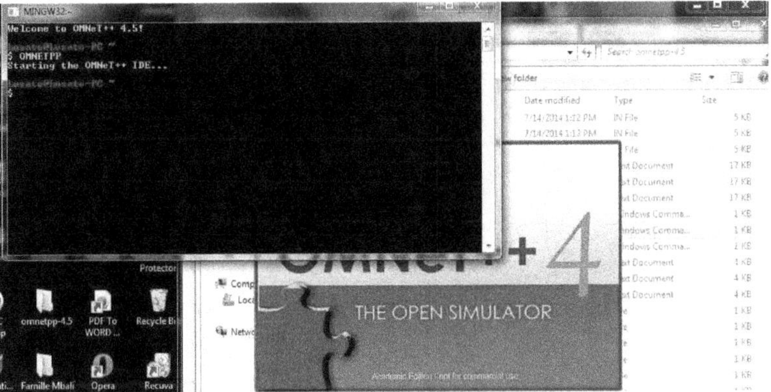

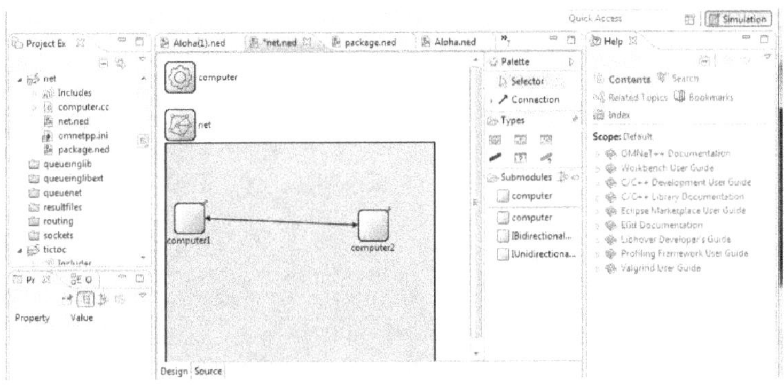